Politics
Today

The Conservative Party

Stewart Ross

Wayland

Politics Today

The Alliance Parties
The Cabinet and Government
The Civil Service
The Conservative Party
Elections
The European Parliament
The House of Commons
The House of Lords
The Labour Party
Local Government
The Monarchy
The Nationalized Industries
The Prime Minister
Trade Unions and Pressure Groups

First Published in 1986 by
Wayland (Publishers) Ltd
61 Western Road, Hove
East Sussex BN3 1JD

British Library Cataloguing in Publication Data
Ross, Stewart
  The Conservative Party. – (Politics today)
  1. Conservative Party – History
  I. Title   II. Series
  324.24104'09   JN1129.C7

  ISBN 0–85078–845–5

Phototypeset by
Kalligraphics Ltd, Redhill, Surrey
Printed in Italy by
G. Canale & C.S.p.A., Turin
Bound in the U.K. by
The Bath Press, Avon

Front cover: Margaret Thatcher, leader of the Conservative Party, speaking at the annual conference.

21115172K

TS

Contents

The Conservative Party

The Conservative Party can trace its history back to the reign of King Charles II (1660–85), making it one of the oldest political parties in the world. Britain has had a Conservative government under Margaret Thatcher since 1979, and there have been eight other Conservative Prime Ministers this century.

All types of people support the Conservative Party, which has over one million individual members. Because it usually prefers to change things slowly, the party is attractive to older people. Many people from the middle classes and

The Conservative Party was formed by the supporters of the King in the reign of Charles II.

4

This contemporary cartoon shows a successful Tory candidate celebrating in the 1852 general election.

the business world, who agree with the party's policies, are also Conservative voters. Some working-class men and women also believe in Conservative policies, particularly those living in the south of England.

When the Conservative Party was formed from the supporters of the King, its opponents called its members 'Tories'. Originally, this was an abusive nickname, but it remains in use to this day. During the late nineteenth and twentieth centuries, the Tories have also been known as the Conservative and Unionist Party, showing their strong support for the union of Britain and Northern Ireland.

The Conservatives have formed many of the governments of Britain, and like to consider themselves 'the natural party of government'. The other parties do not accept this, but Conservative policies have proved to be very successful in attracting the votes of the people.

Centuries of Growth

The original seventeenth-century Tory Party lost popularity in the eighteenth century. The modern party has grown out of the one that re-emerged in the early nineteenth century. As more and more people were given the vote by the Reform Acts of 1832, 1867 and 1884, Benjamin Disraeli (Prime Minister 1868 and 1874–80), and other nineteenth-century Conservative leaders, realized that the party had to change. What emerged was a party with nationwide membership, local branches and a broad popular appeal.

After its reorganization in the mid-nineteenth century, the Conservative Party has remained in

Winston Churchill (left) and Anthony Eden headed strong Conservative governments during the 1950s and early 1960s.

As Prime Minister between 1957 and 1963, Harold Macmillan concentrated on foreign and overseas affairs.

more or less the same form into the latter part of the twentieth century. A long period in power ended with the 1905 general election, and it was not until 1922 that Britain had a Conservative government again. Between then and 1945 the country was governed by a Conservative Prime Minister for all but seven years, although there were a number of coalition governments.

There was another long spell of Tory rule from 1951 to 1964, under Prime Ministers Churchill, Eden and Macmillan. More recently, Edward Heath headed a Conservative administration from 1970–74, before Margaret Thatcher took over as Party Leader in 1975.

The Conservatives claim that the key to their success has not been adherence to rigid principles, but in flexibility. Over the years the party has tried to keep in touch with the mood of the nation, and adapt its policies accordingly.

7

Conservatism

The Conservative Party, unlike Labour, is not bound to a single political system, but has certain guidelines. It regards itself as a national party, representing all British citizens, regardless of their background. Its basic beliefs are those of personal freedom, choice and opportunity.

It is maintained by the party that Conservatism involves looking back, and learning from history and experience; and the understanding of and involvement in the current situation. The party looks forward to the future, by weighing up the measures which must be taken to ensure that the society of tomorrow will be one in which the

The Conservatives think of themselves as a 'caring' party, working to look after the needs of all the people.

people of Britain will wish to live.

The rule of law, and recognition that it is the duty of the government to uphold it, is a high priority to a Conservative administration. Conservatives try to ensure that there is justice for every British citizen. They consider themselves to be a 'caring' party, working to look after the needs of all the people, especially children, the elderly and the disabled.

Free enterprise – that is, rewarding effort, skill and initiative in the business world – is seen by the Conservatives as the best way of creating a healthy economy. They believe that by encouraging free enterprise, the economy should grow, and will then be able to fund improvements that are needed in the social services.

The Conservatives believe that Britain must be able to deter her enemies, and must be able to defend herself in the event of an attack. They regard this as a basic necessity if the other aims of the Conservative party are to be achieved.

The Cabinet contains all the top ministers, who are responsible for carrying out government policies.

Policies in Government

The way the principles of the Conservative Party are put into practice through government policies depends on the leader and on the needs of the nation at the time.

The Conservatives believe that keeping inflation down is the first priority of the government. They try to achieve this through their monetary policies, such as curbing public spending and borrowing. Recently, the government has sold off state-owned businesses, like British Airways and British Telecom, to private ownership, although it has been criticized these moves.

Unemployment is a major concern in Britain at the moment, and would be the first priority of a Labour government, before reducing inflation. The Conservatives have introduced measures to encourage employment, and believe that once Britain emerges from the world-wide recession, many new jobs will be created in private businesses. The Conservatives also wish to raise the

By encouraging children to study science and other more technical subjects, the Conservatives believe they will be better prepared for employment.

Under Conservative administrations, spending on the police force has increased.

standard of education in Britain, placing an emphasis on technology, thus making young people more employable once they leave school.

The Conservatives believe that many people want to buy their own homes, and have given council tenants the 'right to buy'. The government has increased spending on the National Health Service and police force, and believes that more money should be spent on defence. They aim to replace Britain's Polaris nuclear missiles with the new Trident system, and support balanced disarmament.

Under Edward Heath, Britain joined the EEC in 1973. The party is a firm supporter of the Community, although there are those on both the left and right who oppose this policy.

Structure

The structure of the Conservative Party is like a pyramid. The Leader, who heads the Parliamentary Party and the Central Office, stands at the top, and at the base are about one million individual members. A party member belongs to a local Association, and pays a membership fee. All the Constituency Associations are members of the National Union of Conservative and

The Conservative Central Office houses many different departments which carry out important work for the party.

The print unit at Reading publishes material for use by party workers.

Unionist Associations, through which all voluntary helpers work. It runs Area Councils and the Central Office, and also organizes the annual party conference.

Full-time agents work for the party in many constituencies, managing them for a candidate or MP. Above them are eleven Area Offices and the Central Office, at 32 Smith Square, London, SW1. This is run by the Party Chairman, who now also holds a seat in the Cabinet.

Central Office employs about 130 people in several different departments. The Chairman's Organization Department covers areas such as local government, youth and European affairs. Other departments include the Women's Department, which organizes the work of the women in the constituencies; the Training and Campaigning Department, which ensures the party's resources are used most effectively in training agents and during elections; and the Research Department, which provides the party leadership with new ideas for tackling problems. When the party is in opposition, with no access to the Civil Service, this department is vital. There is also a Print and Distribution Centre at Reading, which publishes material for party workers.

Finance

The Conservative Party is wealthier than all the other British political parties put together. In the year 1983–4, the Central Office raised the sum of £9.8 million, and the constituencies collected the same amount for their own use. However, the gap between Conservative and Labour income is narrowing, and at the 1979 general election, the Conservatives were spending millions of pounds more than they were receiving. They were forced to sell the Central Office, and lease it back again.

The Conservatives receive many donations, usually from industry. In the year 1983–4, these totalled £8.7 million, and the constituencies gave

In 1948, the newly-introduced mobile bookshop was used as a publicity device by the Conservatives. They used it as part of membership drives.

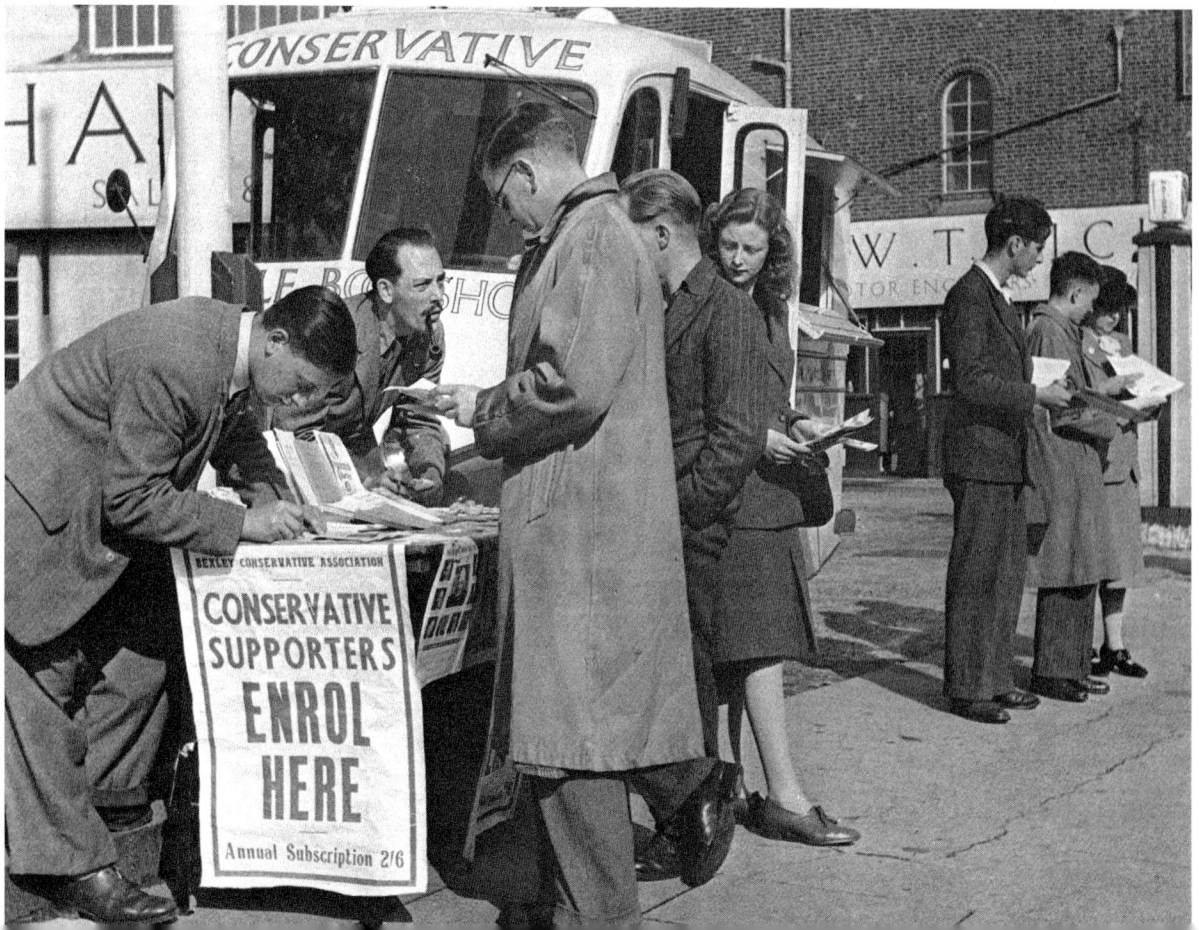

£1.1 million to the Central Office. The membership fee, a minimum of £6, is used by the constituencies, and there are many locally organized events to raise funds for the party, such as wine and cheese parties and jumble sales. 'Mail shots' are carried out occasionally, when the party writes to thousands of possible supporters asking for donations.

The Conservative campaign leading up to the 1983 general election was the most expensive and successful to date.

Over half of all Conservative Party spending is at a local level. The biggest item of expenditure is a general election campaign. In the four weeks before the 1983 election, the party spent over £3.5 million, of which over £2.5 million went on advertising. Many political commentators have said that this Conservative campaign was one of the best organized of recent years.

Conservatives and Business

The Conservative Party believes in individual enterprise, and wants as few nationalized industries as possible. It also tries to keep direct taxation on incomes down, so people can spend their money as they wish. However, it has increased indirect taxation, for example on goods and services through VAT. Many businessmen are attracted to the Conservative cause, and many of the party's MPs have worked in the City before entering Parliament. Margaret Thatcher has encouraged private companies to compete, for example, in the telephone business, which was previously a state monopoly. Since 1979, the Conservatives have introduced over a hundred measures to help the small business sector. They have also limited the power of the trade unions through new legislation.

Many city businessmen are attracted into politics, and may put themselves forward as candidates for one of the parties.

The business world is responsible for many of the largest donations to the Conservative Party. In the year 1983–4, fourteen companies gave over £50,000 each to the party.

A second way in which industry has helped the Conservatives is by coming to an agreement over wages and prices. In 1971, the Confederation of British Industry, an organization of all the major employers, agreed to limit wage and price increases to 5 per cent. As a result of this, inflation fell rapidly.

Some people feel that political parties should not be tied too closely to a single group, such as industry; or the trade unions in the case of the Labour Party. They would prefer the state to fund the political parties, so that they could compete for votes on an equal basis.

The CBI agreed to limit wage increases in 1971 to help Edward Heath's government. It holds an annual conference to discuss policies for the coming year.

The Leader

The position of the leader of the Conservative Party is very powerful. Once chosen, he or she has almost complete control over the party. The leader selects the Party Chairman, who runs the Central Office as he or she wishes. The Cabinet or Shadow Cabinet, if the party is in opposition, is appointed by the leader. The leader also has the final say on policy matters. At the party conference, the Conservative leader has a much easier time than the leaders of the other parties have at their conferences.

In the Conservative Party, the leader is a very powerful figure. As Prime Minister, Margaret Thatcher represents her party's views abroad as well as at home.

18

However, the leader of the Conservative Party cannot simply do what he or she wants. There is machinery for the selection of a leader each year. Usually there is no vote, but if a leader loses the confidence of the party, his or her leadership may be challenged. This happened to Edward Heath in 1975, when he was replaced by Margaret Thatcher. A wise leader, therefore, keeps in touch with the mood of the party, and works with it rather than against it.

The Conservative leader is chosen by the party MPs in the House of Commons. The system of voting is rather complex – three separate ballots may be needed – but in the end the party is sure to have a leader who has been voted for by the great majority of Conservative MPs. This gives the leader confidence as he or she takes the party into the tough political battlefield.

It is important for a leader to keep in touch with the view of the party members and public.

Conservatives at Westminster

The most important Conservative organization in the House of Commons is the '1922 Committee'. All back-benchers belong to this, and they elect their own chairman. The 1922 Committee has an Executive Committee and a number of elected policy committees on subjects such as agriculture and employment. The views of these committees have considerable influence on ministers, especially when the party is in opposition.

Normally MPs vote the way the party leadership wants them to. The wishes of the leader are passed on to MPs by a group of party officers called whips, who are also MPs. It is the job of the whips to make sure that MPs turn up and vote in support

The 1922 Committee of back-benchers carries out important work for the party, covering a wide variety of subjects.

of their party. If an MP ignores the wishes of the whips, he is unlikely to be offered a government post when the party is in power.

After the 1983 general election, the Conservatives had 397 seats in the House of Commons, giving them an overall majority of 144. In the House of Lords, the Conservatives have about 400 peers, out of the 1200 who could attend, who have pledged to support them. Many of the 220 Independents also regard Conservative policies favourably, and only about 200 peers are openly linked with other parties.

A Conservative MP meets with his assistant to discuss the forthcoming day's events in Parliament.

But the extent of the Conservative power in the Commons and Lords is not necessarily a help to the party leadership. Conservative MPs in the Commons have voted against the advice of the whips on several occasions, and, in the 1980s, the House of Lords has rejected Conservative proposals a number of times.

Who Votes Conservative?

The appeal of the Conservative party is broad. In the 1983 general election the party received 42 per cent of all the votes cast, which included almost a third of the votes of trade union members. But the party is strongest among the wealthier, middle-class people, and the result of the 1983 election was really a reflection of the public's lack of confidence in the other major parties at that time.

The heart of Conservative strength is in the

General election campaigns are an important way of attracting votes. These posters were published by the Conservatives for the 1950 election, but they failed to form the next government.

south of England, where the party won almost all the seats in the 1983 general election. On the other hand, it now holds no seats in Glasgow or Liverpool, and is poorly represented in Scotland and Wales.

Older people are attracted to the Tory Party by its conventional policies. The Conservative Party also appeals to many people who own their own house, or work in private industry. The very wealthy generally vote Conservative because they fear that the other parties would increase the amount of tax they pay.

Despite the middle-class appeal that the Conservative Party has, many working-class people have also given it their support. Traditionally, the Labour Party styles itself as the party of the working class. However, it is known that many people are attracted by the 'tough' image of the Conservatives on questions such as law and order, immigration and defence. For example, the resolute attitude of Margaret Thatcher during the Falklands War won her support from many different sections of the British public.

Party Activists

Party workers meet to discuss their ideas and plans for their election campaign, in January 1950.

The Conservative Party is fortunate in that there is a tradition that its helpers serve the party, rather than try to impose their ideas upon it. As in the Labour Party, however, activists are not always representative of those who vote for the party, and the Conservatives have had trouble with them from time to time.

Almost half the Conservative vote is made up of industrial workers of some kind, yet these people do not usually occupy positions of responsibility within the party. People who run their own businesses, on the other hand, make up a tiny fraction of the Conservative vote, yet are very powerful within the party. As a result of this, those who are active in party work are generally less moderate, more right wing, than those who support the party in elections.

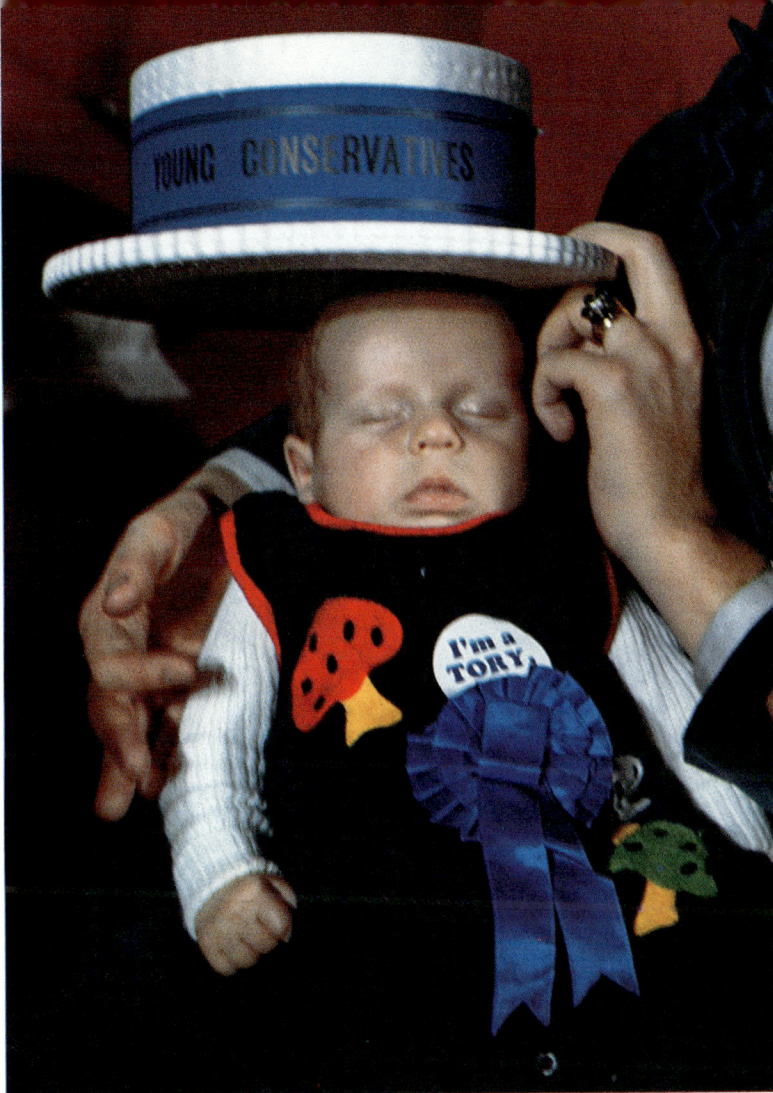

Loyalty to the party can be taken to extremes!

There are many areas of work open to the supporters of the Conservative Party. Candidates have to be found, selected and supported for three types of election: local, parliamentary and European. The National Union has a huge structure, with councils and committees at all levels, all needing volunteers to serve on them. Also, money-raising events need to be organized regularly by volunteer workers.

Finally, there are groups of Conservatives who try to influence the actions of people on specific issues. For example, Lady Olga Maitland's 'Women and Families for Defence' are very active in the support of multilateral disarmament.

Selection of Candidates

One of the major functions of a Conservative Constituency Association is to select candidates to stand in elections. Although the Central Office will advise on procedure, the Constituency Association does this work with a considerable degree of independence. The National Union can refuse to accept an unsuitable candidate, but it has only done this twice since 1945.

The Constituency Association begins the selection procedure by going through a list of names put forward. Some of the people on this list will have been recommended by the National Union.

It is useful if a proposed candidate has a supportive husband or wife. Denis Thatcher is a great source of strength to Margaret Thatcher.

A selection committee is set up at this stage, as there might be a list of as many as 100 names to work through.

This committee usually reduces the number on the list to about twelve candidates. These are interviewed, possibly with their wives or husbands. After this the Constituency Association has to choose between a final short-list of three or four candidates. The selection is normally made by the Executive Council of the Constituency Association. However, in Reigate in 1968 the party invited all its 6,000 members to a meeting where the final two candidates were given a chance to speak, after which all those present voted for the candidate they preferred.

Recently, the Conservative Party has been trying hard to change its wealthy, aristocratic image. To achieve this, candidates from all walks of life have been encouraged to come forward and represent the party.

A successful candidate must be able to show that he has a genuine interest and concern in local matters.

Conference

WE'LL ALL WIN WITH THE CONSERVATIVES.

Every autumn, the Conservative Party holds a conference, usually in a major sea-side resort. At least 5,000 Conservatives from all branches of the party attend. The social functions of the conference are just as important as the political discussions. They help to produce a sense of party unity, and provide one of the few opportunities for constituency workers to meet with the party's leading members.

The practical purpose of the conference is to give the party a chance to debate policy and discuss reports produced by various party groups

Important matters of party policy are discussed at the conference.

during the year. No decisions made at the conference are binding, but are intended to be used as guidelines in the coming year. As well as the main debates on the floor of the conference hall, there are many other meetings arranged, so Conservatives can get together and air their views and plan for the future.

Planning the conference is particularly important because its proceedings are shown on television. The Conservatives have to work hard to ensure that the image of their conference is the right one. The colour schemes are carefully selected, speakers are advised on their dress and delivery, and the more difficult discussions are arranged for the time of day when fewer people will be watching.

The conference is always drawn to a close with a rousing speech by the party leader. This serves to rally the party and send its supporters back to the constituencies eager to continue their efforts for another year.

The staging of the annual conference is important, to give the party the best image possible.

Important Dates

1916   Conservatives join Lloyd George's wartime coalition government.

1922   Conservatives break with Lloyd George and form their own government under Bonar Law.

1923   Stanley Baldwin becomes Conservative Prime Minister.

1931   Conservatives join Ramsay MacDonald's National Government.

1935   Stanley Baldwin becomes Conservative Prime Minister of the National Government.

1940   Winston Churchill, Conservative Prime Minister of wartime coalition government.

1951   Conservatives under Winston Churchill win general election (16 seat majority).

1955   Conservatives under Anthony Eden win general election (60 seat majority).

1957   Harold Macmillan becomes Conservative Prime Minister.

1959   Third consecutive Conservative general election victory (100 seat majority).

1964   Conservatives under Sir Alec Douglas-Home lose the general election.

1965   Edward Heath becomes the first elected Leader of the Conservative Party.

1970   Conservatives under Edward Heath win general election (30 seat majority).

1973   Britain joins the EEC.

1974   Negotiations for a Liberal-Conservative coalition fail after indecisive general election in February. In October, Labour wins general election (3 seat majority).

1975   Margaret Thatcher is elected Leader of Conservative Party.

1979   Conservatives under Margaret Thatcher win general election (41 seat majority).

1982   Falklands War.

1983   Landslide Conservative general election victory (144 seat majority).

Further Reading

Ball, A. R., *British Political Parties* (Macmillan, 1981)

Blake, Lord Robert, *The Conservative Party from Peel to Thatcher* (Fontana, 1985)

Butler, D. and Kavanagh, D., *The British Election of 1983* (Macmillan, 1984)

Coxall, W. N., *Parties and Pressure Groups* (Longman, 1981)

Rose, R., *Do Parties Make a Difference?* (Macmillan, 1980)

Warner, P., *The Political Parties* (Wayland, 1983)

The Conservative Manifesto, 1983

The Conservative Party Information Folder

Glossary

Adminstration   Government.

Back-bencher   An MP not holding a position in the government or shadow cabinet.

Ballots   Votes, usually written down in secret.

Cabinet   The group of leading ministers who advise the Prime Minister.

Candidate   A person who offers himself or herself for a public office.

Civil Service   The many branches of the government service, which are not elected.

Coalition   A group of people from different political parties, working together.

Conference   A meeting of many people for discussions and debates.

Constituency   An area represented by an MP.

Disarmament   Reduction in the number of weapons a country possesses.

Discriminate   Treat differently.

Election   The process by which people are chosen for public office.

Expenditure   The act of using up money and resources.

General election   The election by which MPs are chosen for the House of Commons.

Immigration   The entry into a country of people from other countries.

Inflation   The rate at which prices increase.

Initiative   The first idea or action taken in a matter.

Legislation   Laws.

Minister   An MP holding a government position, but not necessarily in the cabinet.

Monetary   Relating to money and finances.

Monopoly   Total control of a product or service for the public.

Multilateral   On all sides.

Nationalized industry   An industry under the control of the state.

Opposition   The political parties opposed to the government.

Policies   The stated intentions of a political group.

Prime Minister   The elected leader of the government.

Private business   That part of the business world which is run by individuals as opposed to the state.

Radical   Holding extreme political views, and advocating fundamental change.

Recession   A period when the economy is suffering, causing high unemployment.

Right-wing   Conservative; opposed to socialism.

Seat   A place in the House of Commons which an MP takes when he or she is elected.

Shadow cabinet   The cabinet of the opposition.

Social services   The help provided by the state for the less fortunate in society.

Taxation   Money paid to the government.

Trade union   A group of workers from the same field of employment, organized to further its interests in such areas as pay and working conditions.

Voter   A person who may show a choice, as in choosing an MP.

Index

Acknowledgements
The illustrations in this book were supplied by: Camera Press 9, 10, 17, 19, 20, 23, 25; Conservative Party 12, 13; Tony Durant 27; E T Archive 4; Frank Spooner Pictures *cover*, and by the following photographers: K Arkell 29, G de Keerle 26, J Sutton 8, 15, 28; Lloyd's of London 16; Popperfoto 6, 7, 14, 18, 22, 24. All the remaining pictures are from the Wayland Picture Library.

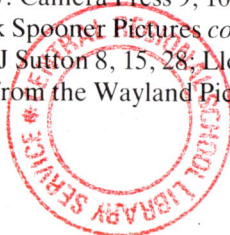